DUTCH TREAT

Rien Poortvliet

DUTCH TREAT

The Artist's Life, Written and Painted by Himself

Harry N. Abrams, Inc., Publishers, New York

Translated from the Dutch
by Maria Milne

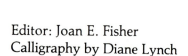

Editor: Joan E. Fisher
Calligraphy by Diane Lynch

Library of Congress Cataloging in Publication Data
Poortvliet, Rien.
  Dutch treat.
  1. Poortvliet, Rien. 2. Illustrators—Netherlands—
Biography. I. Title.
NC983.5.P66A2 1981   759.9492[B]   81-3528
ISBN 0-8109-0818-2   AACR2

Originally published under the title *Van de hak op de tak*
© 1980 Rien Poortvliet
Unieboek BV — Van Holkema & Warendorf, Bussum
English translation © 1981 Harry N. Abrams, Inc.

Published in 1981 by Harry N. Abrams, Incorporated, New York
All rights reserved. No part of the contents of this book may be
reproduced without the written permission of the publishers
Printed and bound in the United States of America

Introduction

When you just draw whatever comes into your mind — the way you have thoughts when you can't get to sleep at night — then this is the kind of picture book that results. Did you ever try to recall such fleeting thoughts? Sometimes they are strange pictures and associations; other times they are glimpses into the past that make you sit up and think, "I haven't remembered that for years!" Quite honestly, I don't have a specific idea for a book — at least not a book with a single subject. There are so many wonderful things for me to draw right here: our dogs and horses, foxes, deer, birds, rabbits, the woodlands, my family, my friends, the people who worked on our house. (We've finally moved into our new house and I can at last use my hands for painting again.) I can even paint from my memory the people I knew and the places I went when I was a boy.

I have an incredible urge to make a book! I'll just start somewhere and see what happens...

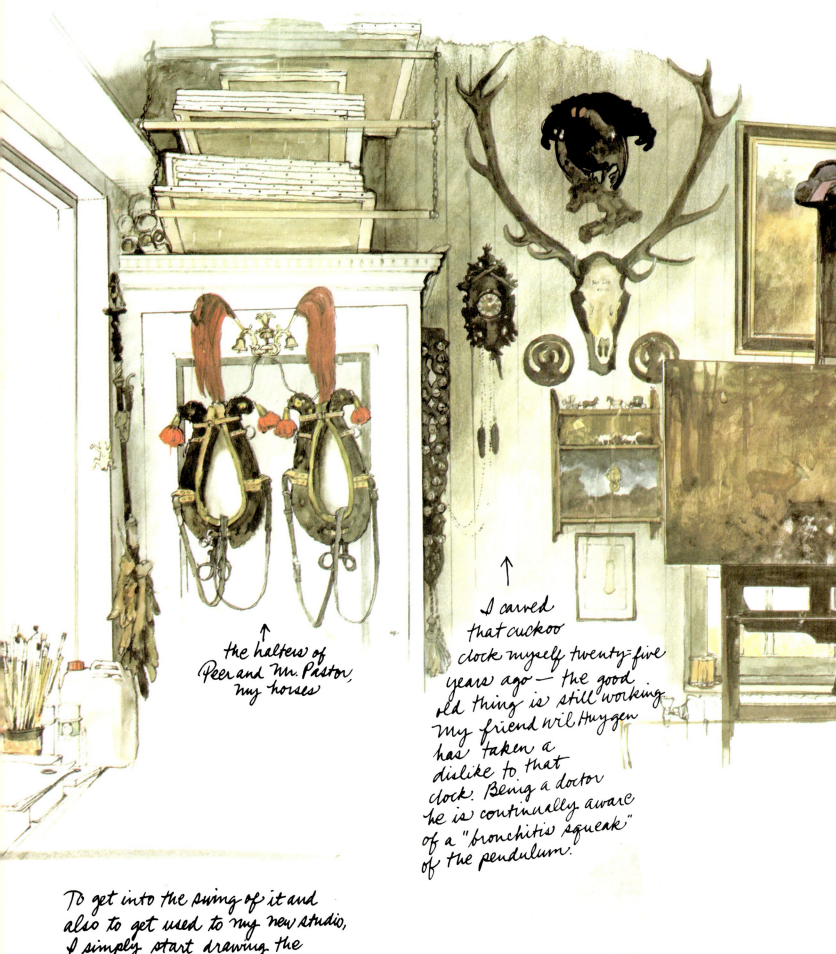

↑ the halters of Peer and Mr. Paston, my horses

↑ I carved that cuckoo clock myself twenty-five years ago — the good old thing is still working. My friend Wil Huygen has taken a dislike to that clock. Being a doctor he is continually aware of a "bronchitis squeak" of the pendulum.

To get into the swing of it and also to get used to my new studio, I simply start drawing the things around me.

This chimney slopes backward. In order to get the moose head to hang straight, a kind of contraption was made by Jan Houtveen, the blacksmith →

I found this old crosscut saw in his workshop. This will come in handy when my son Tok and I cut tree trunks.

In our new yard we have many dead trees that would best be used for firewood.
By rights, I should use horsepower to drag these logs away.

old Dutch seagull

Prijs den HEER met blijde galmen; Gij myn Ziel hebt ryke sto[f]

In the living room there is another fireplace, with a frieze depicting one of the heroic deeds of the kantjil.

In ancient Indonesian tales the kantjil is similar in his slyness to our Reynard the Fox.

A kantjil is a miniature deer about ten inches high; to show you how small this really is I have taken off my slipper, which is exactly twelve inches.

In the zoo there are kantjils behind a large showcase window in lush vegetation. Beautiful! I can watch them for hours. Just imagine having something like that at home!

The Kantjil resembles somewhat the water deer, also a very small animal about knee-high.

We had a male and a female water deer and after two years the doe had three fawns — about the nicest present I ever had in my life.
You couldn't take your eyes off them.
But when the little ones were six weeks old, the mother got sick and died.
This caused us real sorrow.
Fortunately we were able to successfully raise them all, and now they live on a vast fenced-off estate.

Chinese water Deer

At the beginning of this century they were brought to England from China and Korea;

they escaped here and there from parks, and now they run wild in fairly large numbers.

In the winter they have a very thick coat, and their little, deep-set eyes resemble those of a teddybear.

The male water deer has no antlers like a regular roebuck; what he does have are long upper canines.

They never became tame. We never got closer than this.

But I do miss them, and when I look through my window to the wooded area outside, of about eighty by eighty yards, with large old trees (larch, cultivated chesnut, planetree, birch), I can easily imagine them walking around there.

I know that in the not-too-distant future I will ask my wife if it would appeal to her, too; a couple of Chinese water deer in the woodlands.

I would already like to nail a → small feeding rack together!

Through the national conservation organization I bought a bag of wildflower seed that is doing rather well in certain places.

What I have not seen in or around our new house:
 <u>mice</u>...

A pity for our Tim because he is crazy about them!
Even out of his deepest sleep he rears up wildly when you say the word "mice."

The previous house was swarming with mice. In the rabbit run they calmly picked away the food in front of the rabbits' noses.

And as soon as the last chicken went into the night quarters, the mice came out.

They used to climb inside with the canaries and into giji's cage!

They even inhabited the organ in our house; one evening when I was alone I played psalms and hymns as loudly as I could for a whole hour — not so much to praise the good Lord, but to blast away the mice.
They stayed, however.

Then I dismantled the organ and found eight mice!

Timothy eliminated quite a number of them — he moves as fast as lightning!

Very rarely did he miss one.

One week before we moved, Tim caught number five hundred. It was exciting to anticipate that nice round number.

Once in a while Tim made a mistake and caught a field mouse, — which was a shame — I like field mice.

Tim chews on the mouse until it is dead.
 But Manasse, → our youngest dog, holds the mouse gently in his mouth, and when he notices that the other dogs aren't paying any attention to his heroic deed, swallows the whole mouse … alive!

Tim and Manasse are Jack Russell terriers and are sweet little dogs!

Manasse got his name because on the day we got him the Reverend de Jong of Ouddorp had given a rather long sermon about Manasse.

My friend Schriek, gamekeeper in Het Loo, also has a Jack Russell — a bitch, called Witje.

She is such a sweet lap-jumper. Although the Jack Russells I know are nice, it surely doesn't mean they are softies.

It has already happened during three walks with the boss that Witje sneaked away, crept into a foxhole, and there strangled a full-grown fox!

Just imagine that— deep under the ground!

Henk and Alies also have two dogs, Tobias and Jack. Jack is shorthaired.

Arnold Ydwal now has three Jack Russell terriers, besides all his other dogs.

← brother of our Tim

With the help of two of Arnold's terriers → Tok shot his first fox.

For wild boar hunts Jack Russells are used.

For this purpose small dogs are in less danger than big ones.

When a whopper like this makes an upward sweep from below it mows right over the top of such a small dog.

↑ Wirehaired terriers also do that kind of work.

In more or less the same manner as the boar, the roebuck charges from below.

Therefore, a "tame" roebuck, brought up by humans, is very dangerous. Everybody thinks, "Oh, such a small animal," but as fast as an arrow he is right with you!

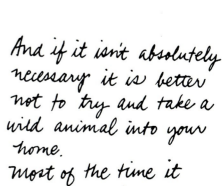

And if it isn't absolutely necessary it is better not to try and take a wild animal into your home.
Most of the time it doesn't work.

Fawns and fox cubs are so sweet. You'd go right down on your knees!

But don't do it — there's already enough messing around with animals.

Once upon a cold December day I found a bedraggled, young hare. With the bottle and oatmeal we got him to eat, and he grew up successfully in the chicken run. But after a year he became "amorous" — he had plenty of food but no females. That's why we set him free in the polder.

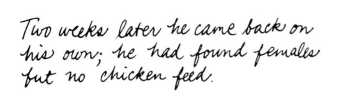

Two weeks later he came back on his own; he had found females but no chicken feed.

When he did not succeed he became mean; screaming, biting, and scratching!

There was nothing else for me to do but to get on the table and wait for his tantrum to subside.

Shrieking, he raced around the table and all the while tried to get on top. I finally had to kick him away!

A couple of friends who happened to drop in thought that I was making a fool of myself. But in no time at all they had joined me on the table — with painful shins.

Behind a pile of junk on top of a cupboard I discovered an ugly old stuffed hare —
I had been missing the thing for years. I lowered it by its ears.

Eight times the hare bred the dusty object until its ear broke off.

Embarrassed, he crawled into his corner.

That evening I took him to a farm in the woods.

There he was seen again often in the early mornings amid the chickens.

Raising members of the crow family is usually very successful.

Our two magpies and our Flemish jay reached the age of fourteen.

The birds would be quite naughty. Often I would find between the pages of my "bedtime" book a piece of wet meat from the dog's bowl.

Our boys scolded those magpies a lot!
While they were concentrating on their homework, a bird would suddenly come sailing through the open window, land, boom! on the table, and disappear again — almost always with a pencil or something like that.

In old age their lives came to an unpleasant end: I found them lying half-eaten in the aviary where they always spent the night.

I put my highseat ladder against a tree and there I waited for nightfall, and yes, there appeared a giant rat!

Bang

I had already taken an enormous dislike to rats. I would rather grab hold of a live fox, if I had to, than a rat.

This reminds me of a disagreeable incident when I was young. I was tramping along the Schie with my little brother Harm and a friend. With a branch I heaved a dead rat out of the water — one whose body had already swollen up into a ball and had some of its tail skin coming off. I swished it onto the road surface exactly in front of a car wheel. I can still hear the "poff" with which it exploded, and I can still see the perplexed face of my little brother with greenish blobs of intestines on his head.

Actually, all these mice-dwelling experiments were done as a replacement for something I would love to have had. This! It would have been so wonderful! Even now I dream of it!
Tiny, live horses.

At the Tip Top Toy Shop I bought everything they had in the way of farm animals with the "Britains" trademark. They are beautiful and no longer produced.

I still have 10 horses, 17 cows, 18 sheep, and 7 pigs... in a box, it is true, but fun nevertheless.

It suddenly occurs to me; there are:

miniature chickens

minature rabbits

miniature goats

miniature horses

but why no miniature cows? That would be fun.

Just imagine if some animal species of giant proportions occurred.

Speaking of very large animals, in Tanzania I was once sitting on a hill by myself watching hundreds of elephants. Nothing but elephants were passing by as far as you could see. I just sat there amazed, with open mouth, wondering how the Good Lord could have created them!

This is what an elephant looks like when he gets angry. From the corners of his eyes he watches what's going on.

Then he swings his trunk and ears.

His last warning is to throw dirt in the air

and if you still don't understand he will come over and explain!

In Kenya, I saw for the first time in my life lions in their natural habitat. It was completely different from seeing them in the zoo.

One day, prophesies Isaiah (65:25), the lion will eat straw like a cow.

Just as the wolf and the lamb will graze together

For the time being the lions that I saw weren't up to that.

I have always been crazy about the beautiful body of the lion.

And when I was sent to bed early I "lioned" for a long time back and forth along the bed.

I also practiced the movements of the elephant's trunk.

When I was a lion my pajama top was tucked into my pants — when I was an elephant, of course, it was not

As soon as I got home I started to copy the head.
←

Afterward my brother Pit stuffed it very nicely.
Clever boy, Pit.
He fed all the boiled off meat to Pedro, my mother's favorite dog, who just happened to be staying with Pit and Lies.
If my mother only knew!

My other brother Harm has a simple way of stuffing animals.
He sews up the head skin,
then pours concrete in it.

A year later Anton van Hooff phones to say that he has another lion — a male! "If possible please only a head with a mane," I had asked. That would have been fine. But when I got there I found that someone had sawed through it below the ribcage! It was gruesomely twisted, half-frozen, and half-rotted (the freezer had been out of order for a week... Anton didn't know that either).

It took several men to drag the colossus into my car. Actually, by then I didn't want him at all — he smelled terrible and wads of hair were coming loose.
But at that point I just couldn't say I don't want him.

A whole lion weighs about four hundred pounds, so you can work out how much two-thirds weighs.

I didn't know how to get rid of this monster.

The stench was unbearable, even with all the windows open.

Because I had to glance behind me several times, I once had to brake sharply and almost got a bash with that enormous claw. I saw it coming toward me in the rearview mirror just in time to dodge it.

I drove straight to "the Stompert"— I desperately wanted to get rid of this thing. I dug a hole, tied a towrope to one leg, and one, two, three pull!

I found it really a bit spooky, and when I crawled into bed a little later I still felt my pulse racing.

Later on, Tok dug up the whole affair to get the teeth.

← 3.7 inches →

Anton has now promised me a wolf, and I have been looking forward to it for a while.

A dead sparrow can occasionally be found in the garden, and I have no problem getting a hare or a pheasant. Such models are of great value to me — one learns so much from them.

It doesn't take much to please me.

Yesterday Tok saw a skunk that had been killed by a car — he often brings such things home for me.

People who work along the railroad tracks find things for me, too.

And when I shoot a duck I would rather use it as a model than as poultry.

When Corrie has gone to the church choir in the evening I sometimes make drawings of Sep, Max, Tim, and Manasse.

This morning I was not able to continue working on my book as planned. Over the telephone I learned that I must take a shooting test! I dislike abandoning my work, and, although I can shoot quite well, I find it disturbing to have to demonstrate my skill for a bunch of observers sitting on folding chairs behind me.

I was lucky. All five in the red. I was allowed to leave immediately.

Someone who came before me had a good score but failed! This is silly, because after each one of these shots a boar would have dropped dead instantly.

You might say, "Very well, but before you get involved in hunting first show how you shoot." I fully agree. But what I don't understand is why I have to take that shooting test every year. Drivers' licenses are renewed all the time without a test.

I shoot two or three boars per winter and for that I have to obtain a new license each year, but anyone, without taking an exam, can quietly keep hundreds of pigs or chickens in a feedlot together and commit other kinds of gross mismanagement of animals.

For example, on Ameland some years ago I saw this poor devil. The very closely packed herd behind him and the wall before him forced the animal to look either to the right or to the left, which made a dirty semicircle on the wall. Though it happened long ago, the picture of it still keeps me awake sometimes. Something like this always leaves a vivid impression on me.

An image that also haunts me is the wise, accusing look of a gorilla behind bars — it always embarrasses me.

It doesn't bother me with a hippopotamus or a buffalo.

On the Isle of Jersey there is a gorilla-breeding station that distributes young gorillas over Africa.

I once stood there an entire afternoon watching a giant who stared steadily past me off into the distance, and absent-mindedly, with one finger, moved a piece of excrement back and forth.

And when some idiot would come along cracking cheap jokes, I would get furious!

Tok at the zoo.
He could already read a bit,
and after some effort he had figured out what was written on the sign.
 Well, this really made him laugh scornfully:
"Lynx or Los — they don't even know themselves!"

Years later Tok worked in the zoo as summer help, driving the little train and in between the rides selling tickets at the window.
 Directly opposite the window is the Ape House. There he saw one day one of the many chickens that have the run of the place scratching for worms near the cages.

And yes – the monkey made a quick grab for the head, put one foot against the bars to get better leverage

and bye-bye chicken!

My brother Karel, who worked in a pet shop, once did the same thing, accidentally. Out of a large cage with a lot of birds he had to catch one for a woman who kept giving him instructions: "Now it's flying to the left, now it's the third from the right."

When Karel finally caught the right bird and slowly pulled his arm out of the cage, the door dropped down just a little too early.

"Oops, that's not a good one," Karel said, and put it away on a high shelf.

That chicken without a head reminds me of the rooster that my father almost slaughtered. The food shortage was so terrible that I don't know how we managed to feed them until they were full grown, but in 1944 we had three adult roosters on the balcony. When they were big enough, one was meant for the pot.

My father, being no hero in such matters, had appointed me assistant butcher.

my father

We would do it this way:

My father would hold the rooster between his legs, the head in his left hand, the big knife in his right. To keep things well under control I had to hold the legs from the back. That part went well.

It took a long time before my father had gathered enough courage. Suddenly he started sawing like a madman. Of course I couldn't see anything but I could feel rather accurately what was going on.

"Abie, aboe," my father said and I let go. It would have been better if I hadn't done that. →

I remember that I thought this to be a miserable task, but now I would welcome doing any job at all together with my father.

I first saw Mootje (Blackie) as he was walking on the railway platform in Dirksland, on the island of Overflakkee and Goeree. Uncle Dirk was putting me on the steam tram after a stay at his place in the country.

"Look, this is for you," said Uncle Dirk as he put the creature on my arm. It was a cute little animal and I was really very pleased with it, but without a basket or a leash it became a troublesome travel companion. And in those days it was a long journey from Dirksland to Schiedam. First was the steam tram to Middelharnis, where the boat to Hellevoetsluis was waiting — it was a real steamboat, one that would be well suited to carry Saint Nicholas. (The Dutch Santa Claus arrives from Spain on December 5 by boat). Now when I rinse my brush in the canning jar I hear exactly the same "tinging" sound that boat always made. And I can still recall the special smell of the boat.

When you compare this to the dull buses we have now...

During the crossing in those days you still could observe the seals.

At the dock at Hellevoetsluis there was again one of those cute little steam trams, which took you to Rotterdam.

That was some journey! When you finally arrived home it really seemed that you had traveled quite a distance! Now when we drive to Goeree and Overflakkee it takes us a little over one and a half hours from Soest. Convienient of course — but not very interesting.

Then I saw German soldiers.

At first I found them fascinating — I couldn't stop looking: that boot-stamping; how they marched singing in the streets; that strange shouting language. I recall exactly the peculiar musty smell they had. But gradually I took a dislike to them, and I remember exactly the moment I began to hate them.

My father and I were lugging home a piece of wood that looked like a railroad tie.

Suddenly a soldier loomed up!

The brute started making a terrible scene shouting, swearing, threatening. And my father stood there looking thin, pale, meek, with a face of "I will never do it again, Sir."

But the wretch carried on and on. Standing with legs widespread he must have enjoyed his Mussolini imitation.

If I ever met that fellow again...

And even now if at the border the officials make irritating hand gestures, it brings it all back.

That cap!

But, altogether, my childhood during the war was of course quite a fascinating one!

I enjoyed all the secrets that we shared at home together. Nobody on earth would ever have suspected when they saw me walking down the street that we had a radio hidden at home secretly!

And even if they tortured me, I knew absolutely nothing of illegal newspapers. Closed as a clam!

Some boys combed their hair over their forehead like this ↓ and put a pocket comb under their nose, but having that radio at home, I found such gestures going too far.

Then there was another joke: On the ends of two matchsticks we put a round piece of paper.

Then we put them in our fists like this, wound a handkerchief around it, mumbled a bit by moving the ring finger, and said: "Soon we'll be looking like this if the Krauts keep stealing our food."

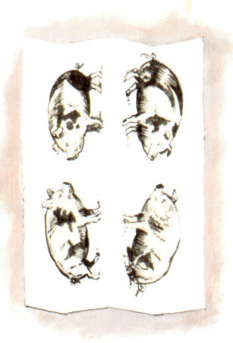

This piece of paper we kept in a dresser drawer. It was called "find the fifth pig" and after some folding you got this head.

The occupation of our school was an act of brazen impudence, I thought.

Still, I had some warm feelings for their horses — those poor devils were victims too.

Krauts were scoundrels. That was one thing we were sure of. But this certainty wavered when a German officer bent over me like the Good Samaritan.

I was almost ten years old, and on the way home from school I had stopped for a moment to look at the beautiful stuffed elk's head that was hanging in a bicycle shop.

I was crazy about that head and often stood there looking at it.

Just behind me a truck loaded with long tubes had to brake to make the turn onto the Rotterdam dike, and I jumped on top of it to get a free ride.

Just around the corner I started to slide down and got my right leg caught under the back wheels.

To straighten out my leg again Dr. Meyer put a sewing machine on it every other day. I thought this to be quite some horse remedy. It did hurt considerably, but it worked.

This reminds me of another simple method.

An elderly ear-nose-and-throat doctor, whom I once met on a hunting trip, judged by the sound of my voice that it was necessary to remove my tonsils. He wanted to do it himself and I didn't dare say no because he had more or less promised me that I would inherit his small hunting ground.

I was tied, hands and feet, to a kitchen chair and then it was simply a matter of stubbornly pulling with a pair of forceps.
Later I learned he hadn't done this kind of work for about fifteen years. The good man has passed away a long time ago — the hunting ground I never got.
Since that time I have been in the hospital only once. While watching a distant roebuck from a tall tree I slipped and an enormous splinter penetrated my skin in a place where I didn't like at all.

It continued to hurt and a week later when I hobbled into Arnold's cabin, my friend Wil said, "Let's have a look." After all, he is a doctor. Arnold lit the area with his flashlight.

"You better have that removed in the hospital," said Wil.

Even though you just go in for a minor, simple operation, this is the outfit you must wear: pajama jacket, underpants, and then those silly stockings.

When you go to the operating room you have to be wheeled even though you can walk perfectly well. Because the bed was too short for me an extension was added, which they once made for Pierre Jansen. But the thing wouldn't fit into the elevator. While I spun around they made every possible attempt to park it in there — no go, so in the end I had to get off the bed anyway.

I recall still another visit to the hospital, when I went for a checkup or something like that.

Afterward I got quite angry: in one of those small closets in a waiting room I had to fill a jam jar with urine and then place it in a hatch.

But where had they put the hatch?

↖There!

On my way out I saw an old lady leaving one of those closets with a jam jar and a bright red face! And she didn't even know what she really looked like...

Often you had to stand in line for hours.

Fortunately, I got over it, but in those days I disliked women. They could sneak in front of you so insidiously — pretending that while chatting they didn't notice they were moving ahead! So there I stood, outraged in between those corset-clad bodies, angry with myself because I couldn't do anything about it!

But what a joy when you finally got your stuff in your bag! It could also happen that it was sold out before it was your turn.

For several reasons when I had to walk along "Lange Haven" I took that side. In the first place it was sunnier there, and second I passed the statue of the gray stallion.

Christian Mission

But the most important reason was that I didn't want to pass the Christian Mission — I had once stolen something there.
Every week we had confirmation classes with Minister Vonk and each time I saw this little kitten on a dark landing. It was made of celluloid and was holding on with his front paws to an empty aquarium. Nobody seemed to own it and I was crazy about the way it was made: the natural posture, those muscles — beautiful!
So one day I snatched it and took it with me.
But after a week I felt so sorry that I secretly hung it back onto the dirty aquarium.

I would have liked to keep it.

For a long time I believed that this was the temple that Samson pulled down (and was probably rebuilt later, or something like that).

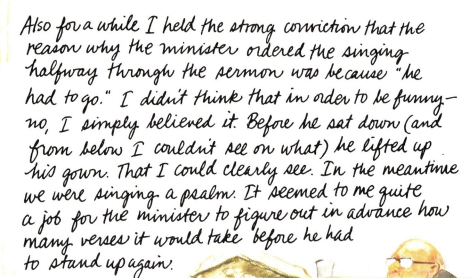

Also for a while I held the strong conviction that the reason why the minister ordered the singing halfway through the sermon was because "he had to go." I didn't think that in order to be funny — no, I simply believed it. Before he sat down (and from below I couldn't see on what) he lifted up his gown. That I could clearly see. In the meantime we were singing a psalm. It seemed to me quite a job for the minister to figure out in advance how many verses it would take before he had to stand up again.

I envied that glass → of water he had — after all, I was dying of thirst too.

Behind the deacons, ← there was always a stern-looking woman who never moved.

I thought her profile would be perfect to put on a coin.

I verified that by looking at her once more through one of the holes of a loose button: yes, precisely.

I have, in church, always enjoyed watching people desperately struggling to stay awake. And I still find it fascinating. They arch their eyebrows very high and try, in this way, to pull up their eyelids.

Once in Flakkee I reveled in watching some of these church brothers in the Elders' pew. The one in the middle just couldn't keep his eyes open, and was constantly dozing off against his neighbor's shoulder. This the man didn't like at all, so what do you think he did? Pretending to have a cold he suddenly shot forward in order to cough, whereupon the sleepy head tumbled into the pew behind the other's broad back.

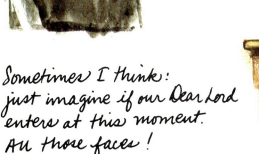

Sometimes I think: just imagine if our Dear Lord enters at this moment. All those faces!

This happened three times during the service.

Even after returning the Christian Mission's kitten I remained thievish. You <u>had</u> to. "The Lord's kindness knows no limits," and, whoops, another post got wriggled free from the barbed-wire barrier. Fuel for the stove. That was quite exciting work!

A real daring trick was to snatch a piece of bread from the Krauts, and then tear off at breakneck speed!

Often I dragged big branches home.

I took those branches out of Plantage Park.

There were other boys who without a qualm broke up the wood from the park benches.

This lion was standing a short distance from the bandstand. When you peered behind the coat-of-arms you could see that the sculptor had not done his work sloppily. It was very clearly a male lion.

Overschie Road

Under the undershirt you wore a "woolly," also knitted.

When I was very, very small the woolly had buttons on the bottom seam.

With a piece of elastic, stockings were attached to it. I hated it — girlish.

Another well-meant knitted absurdity made by Grandma de Boer

The way that scoundrel stared at me at night! I got up screaming.

The beast was about three feet high.

Another time during the night something else frightened the life out of me. At the second-hand market I had bought with my savings a stuffed monkey. I put him on top of a closet so that I could see him clearly from my bed. In that mysterious zone between waking and sleeping I thought I saw something strange… and indeed, his tongue was moving from one side of his mouth to the other, slowly, and without a sound! I was frozen with fear. Only after a long interval did I have courage to get closer… and found that a night moth was fluttering back and forth in the open mouth.

I had a sailor's suit like this. You got a wooden whistle with it, but after the first day it never worked again.

Short pants were baggy in those days.

I looked forward longingly to the first cool autumn day — then I put on my riding breeches, which I liked.

With it went the boy-scout belt with purse and pocketknife.

When you got a bit older you wore the plus-fours, also called "turd catcher."

Then it came time to comb your hair back. That wasn't too successful in the beginning.

There was substitute tea, substitute coffee, pudding, even substitute leather. A satchel made from substitute leather looked good when it was new, but after a few showers it had the appearance of oatmeal. I also had one made of canvas — very sturdy, but of ridiculous dimensions.

I always liked to linger on the bridge to see the ships — I liked to see the skipper swear when I almost spat on his head.

This man had to have five cents otherwise he wouldn't let you into Overschie!

I still remember that.

I thought that the bridge man had to make his living from whatever he collected in the tin cup on his fishing rod.

Someone with meager talent had designed this war money for us. Made of zinc.

The starvation winter was also a severely cold one. Every night our Harm dragged three cushions of a so-called Liberty chair from the storage space. He put those heavy things on his bed and slept beneath them.

The Germans were wretches but I liked this design very much. This dilemma I found hard to stomach as a child.

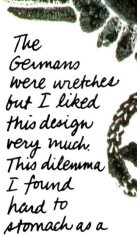

There was so much to see

and always the droning of airplanes.
↓

Before the distribution, Grocer Den Hollander used to sit on guard all night with a giant bouvier.

(I never understood how he managed to keep such a big hungry animal alive.)

God's gift from heaven — Swedish white bread. Never before had I eaten anything as delicious as this!

Those "welfare biscuits" came in these military-looking tins.

One day I saw Jan Scharloo on a sandbar called "The Boezem." He was constructing a raft using sixteen of those tins. He hadn't told me anything about that! And by the look of it he didn't do too badly — he had tied the whole business together with old bicycle innertubes. And sure enough, there he was crossing the lake without a hitch!

It took about half an hour before he came back. I wanted to try it so badly, but, oh no, he didn't tire of it for quite a while. Green with envy, I could do nothing but stand there and watch.

But then, justice! In the middle of the lake the whole affair burst apart, tossing the tins up to the sky just like matchboxes held together too tightly with an elastic band. Fantastic!

Half-swimming, half-wading, and without turning his head once, Jan got to the other side. I have never seen anything as spectacular since.

In that water you could catch loads of tadpoles in the spring.

For salamanders you had to go to the farm ditches; you simply swished a wad of duckweed and algae out of the water onto the land and you would always spot a few.

Catching sticklebacks was even simpler — you tied a worm onto a string; not even a hook was used. Often you caught two fish at the same time.

We often played outdoors — there weren't as many toys as there are nowadays.

On the landing we had a swing.

You really had to steer straight because you needed to go right through the door opening.

Dad made this game for us out of cardboard. You had to stick the safety pin into the carpet and with your index finger you made the string vibrate. It worked very well.

But never mind all this folly. — Yesterday I visited my friend Koen when I heard the news that Queen Juliana was going to abdicate! That was quite a shock for us!

Our queen being no longer our queen, this really will take some time for me to get used to.

The first time I saw our queen at close quarters was when she and the prince entered the palace on the Dam in '53. I was a sentry of the palace, together with my bunkmate Jim van de Ruijt. I was not able to see Her Majesty that well because I stood there "presenting arms," and then of course you have to look straight ahead. So it was only out of the corner of my eye that I saw her.

Being on display like this for the Dutch public you could not of course muddle around.

We had exercised seriously: carefully counting forty steps and then a simultaneous turnaround right. This has to be done with style.

More than twenty years later in that same palace the prince decorated me with the Silver Carnation.

I still have that sailor's cap.

The nice thing is that our Tok wore my twenty-five-year-old cap during his service — that was really an "old-boy's cap."

When you first enter the service the cap looks like this and all hell would break loose if you tinkered with it!

Only toward the end of the service would it sit comfortably.

During the summer months we wore a white cover on top. We always looked forward to that. It made the whole appearance brighter. But the disadvantage was that you had to wash it so often.

You'll always see marines picking up something in this manner. If they bent over in the normal way their cap would drop onto the deck.

In the Navy you never say "ground" or "floor" but always "deck." "Let's hear those heels on deck!" the exercise officer always shouted. And you were just walking in the town square! A man like that does not say "attention" (geeft acht), but:

...for a moment nothing...   YAWNS

Here it looks as if he is still thinking about it. This is misleading.

He suddenly sounds terribly angry! His hands stretch out so fast that his fingers turn upward.

← The dress collar is still in my possession

You probably thought that this collar was attached to a shirt, but it isn't. I'll show you how such a sailor suit is put together.

The "bib" is attached to the straps of the undershirt. For this we used ordinary pennies.

So when you undressed at night you put your two cents next to your pile of clothes.

The next garment is a black pullover that does have an attached collar.

One morning I discovered that the picture of the queen had disappeared from my pennies! What happened? Kessie Kovel's drunken head had been sick over them during the night.

← The queen... gone just like that!

This pullover was so tight that you could hardly take it off by yourself.

A square, black silk cloth is rolled up very tightly.

You make a knot in the middle ↓ and then tie the ends together →

This neckerchief is worn underneath the black collar. →

When you went ashore and on Sundays and holidays, you wore the dress collar over the black collar. The dress collar is attached to your trouserbelt with shoelaces.

In the winter we wore a duffel jacket, and the dress collar was supposed to go over the jacket collar. This is the way to do it: bend over and flip the collar upward. But then, that's not all because there again the black collar of the pullover has to be *under* the jacket! That you pull into place like this.

underwear, socks, blankets, gloves, scarf, boiler suit, jacket, raincoat, bibs, sportswear, etc., etc. There seemed to be no end to it.

You had to have your Navy number on every part of your gear. It took me a full week to embroider 87900 in chain-stitch.

87900

A marine has to take care of his outfit — washing, mending, sewing, etc. Honestly, I just don't want to be bothered with that — that's how I feel about it. When I went home on leave my mother did the laundry. Later, at sea, I had to improvise:

a shirt with a seam undone I repaired with a stapler;

for putting on buttons I used half a paperclip;

With a tube Prussian blue and some white paper I made my own throwaway bibs.

Mending I didn't do out of principle. After three months my socks looked like this, but the high shoes that I wore on board came to here, so nobody noticed.

During that time I didn't wash them either — I would be out of my mind to do such a thing.

At such times I thought there was a lot of disregard for the comfort of the common sailor. It was typical, for example, that you'd find two shoe brushes with your outfit but no pajamas. When a sailor turned in he just had to do that in his underwear.

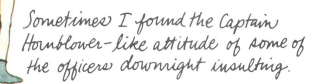

Sometimes I found the Captain Hornblower-like attitude of some of the officers downright insulting.

"IS THAT YOUR HABIT, BUMPKIN, TO PEEP INTO THE OFFICERS' CABINS?"

I had to deliver a cable somewhere in that gangway and through the officer's window I saw strangely painted houses gliding past! So that's what Canada looks like...

As if the miserable cabin of that wretch interested me one little bit! But a "third class" is not allowed to answer back.

A day or so later in the harbor of Montreal, the light was suddenly switched on in the crew's quarters.
A brand-new lieutenant enters showing his visitors how the folks from below deck are situated.
And you are lying there, at eye level, on display. I couldn't think of anything better to do but to pretend I was asleep.

I won't forget this insult as long as I live.

At the Navy training center a quartermaster instructed us in the art of "berth-lashing."

A hammock has to be lashed so tightly that in an emergency it can be used as a life preserver.

When I was placed on the H.M. Doorman, I found there was only one hook.

The other end had to be fastened to the stairs. That was a nuisance because my weight lifted the stairs slightly off the ground and when somebody used the stairs I was shaken up and there was a thumping sound.

BOING BOING

oars-up

Part of the basic training was learning to row at sea.
"Pull-up together."
I liked this very much.
At first I thought that "oars up" (a kind of standing at ease) would be pleasant. But you find out soon enough: the icy cold water runs down and finds its way into the blisters on your hands, and then further into your sleeves.

During the lessons on splices and knots I paid careful attention. This knowledge is still useful to me – eye-splicing, halter ropes, traces, piece of string behind the mail slot, and more.

The rest of the training didn't appeal to me — they made me a telegraph operator. I don't understand anything about transmitters and I have no talents in that direction whatsoever. All that "dit-dotting" drove me nuts.

At a quarter to four in the night I had to get out of my hammock and then immediately put those panicky earphones on my sleepy head!

In those days I had to serve twenty-one months, eight of which were spent on the H.M. Karel Doorman.

It is always somewhat stuffy on board and there is a constant smell of oil.
It was delightful to catch a breath of salty, fresh air.

From this spot I saw a lot of beautiful things: with my own eyes I saw a spouting whale!

← and playing porpoises

and once an enormous shark!

When we were off duty we sometimes went to watch the activities on the flight deck. The landing didn't always happen faultlessly. With a hook the plane had to catch one of the brake cables.

And if it missed, it had to pull up as quick as lightning.

That was not always successful...

and it happened once that it plunged into the sea just before the bow. The ship clattered over it in its full length. You could hear the thumping — to my surprise the flight crew came on board unscathed.

Once I had that large flight deck all to myself! It was a pity though that the weather was very bad, and to be quite honest I wasn't there for my pleasure. I had been put on punitive exercises — one hour.

I got my orders shouted at me from the tower " to the right... left".
I was punished because I had forgotten to close the padlock on my locker. That's why.

During those months when I was serving on the Doorman we were sometimes in heavy weather with strong gales. Being the substitute organist I played on those occasions before the service began:

"Oh Lord please hear our prayers for those in distress at sea."

(the organ was screwed down)

Notwithstanding, the church folks got flung together in one heap.

This is what happened when we entered the services: "Catholics, step out!" — the remaining group is Protestant.

A meal during a gale was not without excitement either. Such a big mess table shoved into your stomach makes quite an impact, and then hot pea soup in your lap as well. But what do you expect? Metal legs on a metal deck slide very easily.

Every week we ate pea soup... standing order. Summer, winter, in the sweltering heat in the Mediterranean, when it was suffocatingly hot beneath the flight deck — it didn't matter. This has been done for centuries.

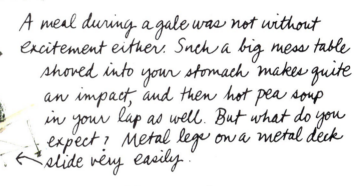

If we liked to eat potatoes with our warm meal we had to peel them ourselves after breakfast.

Later on the sailor could collect the nets with boiled potatoes.

When you looked into the potato shed after a few weeks at sea you saw some very weird things.

A few of us were lying in the sick bay suffering from scurvy!

I thought that was funny... just like in the old days.

On Sundays we sometimes got an orange or an egg. Then there was a long line in front of the galley hatch.

My mate, Tom Brugman, was very wily at that! In the crush of people it just looked like a hand of someone who was being pushed out of line.

He always got two.

When we were allowed on land in Morocco we stocked up on loads of fruit.

But oranges or not, Sunday was always a festive day because we had **rijsttafel** (an Indonesian dish consisting of rice, to which a wide variety of meats, vegetables, fish, fruits, condiments, etc., are added) — and that is by itself reason enough to prefer the Navy.

On one occasion, however, I could not pay that much attention to the rijsttafel. In Canada Chief Poking Fire and his people had been invited to dinner on board. There were long tables in the hangars. Thank God I had drawn a lucky number — my table companion was an Indian woman, 84 years old — thus born in 1870. I watched her all during dinner. How is it possible — she had experienced the real Indian times.

In spite of the rather dull but fast trip, we have been spending our vacations at Ouddorp, a village on Goeree and Overflakkee, for eighteen years running, and whatever the weather is like we amuse ourselves excellently.

After the first sunbathing we let ourselves get covered in sand on the beach and have a game of croquet as the dogs roam nearby.

As long as we are playing Max stands in a shallow pool and barks away at shrimp and whatever is moving in the water — he's been doing that for about ten years.

Sep we have to watch a bit; he has the habit of lifting his leg over the equipment of some lone fisherman.

In the afternoon Corrie stays home with the small dogs and Tok and I go pigeon hunting on Jan van der Baan's property.

One of the small cottages at the dike was inhabited by a person who, from time to time, placed a couple of inflated garbage bags on top of the dike. There were ghosts in them — he had caught them in the night!

At this creek we sometimes waited for the migrating ducks.

When hunting Sep looks like this all the time,

and like this when there is a plate of cookies on the table.

He has been stealing lately and I will have to lie in wait for him.

We love the wide open landscape of Flakkee and the big skies; when you live in the woods you don't see much of that. We are crazy about these picturesque towns too. Sometimes all you can hear is the practicing of the local brass band.

A corner in Goedereede.

While I am drawing this I am thinking:
"Who on earth would get it in his stupid head to put such an ugly telephone booth in such a lovely spot?"

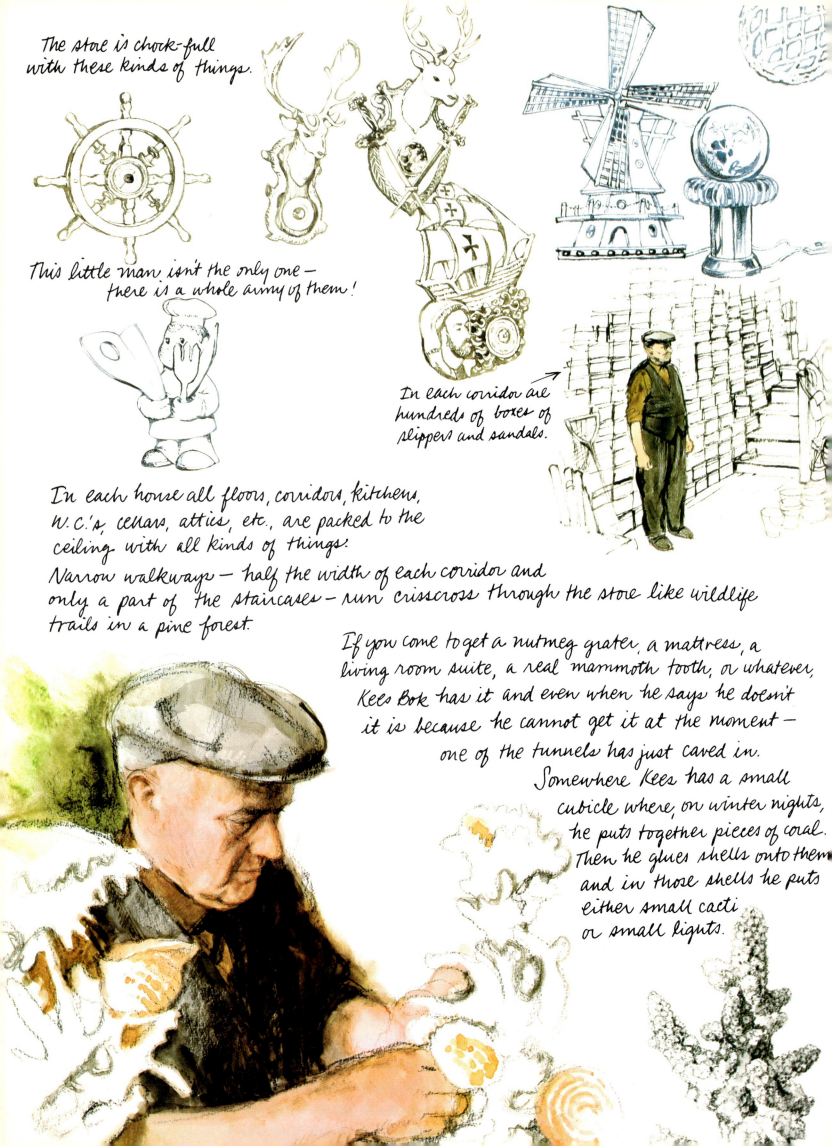

The store is chock-full with these kinds of things.

This little man isn't the only one — there is a whole army of them!

In each corridor are hundreds of boxes of slippers and sandals.

In each house all floors, corridors, kitchens, W.C.'s, cellars, attics, etc., are packed to the ceiling with all kinds of things.
Narrow walkways — half the width of each corridor and only a part of the staircases — run crisscross through the store like wildlife trails in a pine forest.

If you come to get a nutmeg grater, a mattress, a living room suite, a real mammoth tooth, or whatever, Kees Bok has it and even when he says he doesn't it is because he cannot get it at the moment — one of the tunnels has just caved in.
Somewhere Kees has a small cubicle where, on winter nights, he puts together pieces of coral. Then he glues shells onto them and in those shells he puts either small cacti or small lights.

Kees gets those mammoth teeth from fishermen who sometimes find them in their nets.
I hope to get another one from him — I like such venerable old objects.

These objects I got from the amateur archeologists club of Goeree and Overflakkee "de Motte."

This is an eighteenth-century drinking bowl or chafing dish, a so-called ringeloor.

The other one is a porridge bowl from about 1675.

To be able to own objects with history behind them has significance for me.
For example, that porridge bowl — once upon a time there must have been a sulky child sitting behind it, while the mother admonished: "I warn you — you are not going out until you have finished your porridge!" And then to hold that same bowl in my hands, three centuries later! That gives me a thrill.

I also have a stone that is precious to me. It comes from the ruin in Schiedam, where I was born and raised.
As a small boy I always found it fascinating to walk past the ruin...
   Also a little spooky,
      especially in the dark.

It grieved my youthful heart that that wonderful structure was allowed to deteriorate. One dark night I gathered my courage and went to steal a stone; with something tangible like that in my hands it was easier to fantasize.

← This pleases me very much too: a nice old bible from 1768.

Maybe one of these churchgoers was carrying my — or rather, his book under his arm.
What an idea that we, he in the past and I in the present time, are singing the same psalms:—
"How lovely is thy dwelling place,
 O Lord of hosts!
Blessed are those who dwell in thy house,
 ever singing thy praise!"   (Psalm 84)

← Harm and Wieke live in a small wooden house at the end of this path. ↓

I can't thank the Good Lord enough for the marvelous profession I have.
But sometimes I am just a tiny bit envious of people who make music.

For example, when I hear Teke Bijlsma playing Psalm 119...

With this backhoe Honkes can take "big bites."

↑ Honkes dug a six-foot-deep trench straight across the woodlands (the house had no sewerage system) and when he had filled it in again I planted grass there to make a nice grazing path.

At Bos's, →
our village timber merchant
I bought wood for a shed.

garbage-can shed   night house for the chickens   chicken run

Since the road is quite a distance from the house I use this milkcart for the garbage cans.

← In the back wall of the garbage-can shed I sawed a small spy hole so that I would be able to view the sixty-yard-long grazing path through the woodlands and observe the animals!

This, I think, is really the nicest aspect of the whole shed.

This thing also comes from Bos; → when there is a strong wind the little man works like crazy! The turning vanes cause the fellow to work — that I understand, of course — but still I always see it the other way around.

In earlier days my father made something similar — two little guys sawing, though I've forgotten how exactly it worked — something like this →

It was quite some undertaking when the colossal thing was being hoisted onto a truck.

But the transportation went off without a hitch.

Looft, looft den HEER.

I had wanted to paint these words on the tower but Niek, our contractor (and church elder), considered this just a bit too bold.

This transportation didn't go so well.
At the sawmill I bought thirty posts to fence off the woodlands (the Chinese water deer!).
Just past the Echo Well where the road suddenly dips steeply, the load began to shift. I spun around three times over both sides of the road! The trailer (borrowed from Niek) was completely wrecked. Apart from that nothing happened — Praise the Lord!

I still have this road post

I am looking at all the objects that have suddenly come whirling past my window. (I've already brought a few of these indoors), and one thing is clear: autumn. That means it's about time to start working in the woodlands. Mr Douesteyn has already felled a few trees.

The felled trees are allowed to remain where they have fallen, on top of those four hundred dead little Christmas trees. They make excellent cover for birds and other animals.

Speaking of birds, those pheasants with clipped wings (four hens and one cock) indeed arrived, but it didn't turn out the way I expected.

Five days after we had put them out in the chicken run, we saw them walking on the outside, and when we tried to catch them, they flew away over our house without any trouble!

"I don't understand this at all," said the man from whom I had bought them. No, neither do I.

Sometimes I see one of them scurrying around near the automatic feeder.

If they would learn how to tap against the bucket, feed would be released. But, because they are too stupid for that, a ring of corn kernels has been attached, and they certainly do peck against these!

But what did I see a day or two ago? My pheasant cock, dead and partly eaten, had been pulled into an underground burrow either by a rat or a skunk!

Tok sat there until dark with his rifle cocked, but saw nothing. If it is a rat, it has to go, but a skunk I still find quite interesting.

That turned out to be quite some winter! Toward the end the wildlife was starving to death. Every other day I got two crates of stale bread at Rademaker's. Using a sled I left these around the flax fields; when I returned with the next load it would be gone.

I made deliveries at the homes of rabbits I was aquainted with and then dropped off a variety of goods — there was a wide choice: wholewheat bread, white bread, currant bread, French bread, croissants, coffee cakes, etc.

"Just give me a mixture, baker."

The buzzards were already waiting.

Every year in January there is an event that makes me especially cold: the foxes' mating season. I sit up in a tree at night waiting to see the foxes. With snow on the ground and especially when there is a full moon you can see quite clearly.

I barely manage to climb into that tree because I feel like a stuffed sausage with all these clothes. And once I get there I must sit as still as a mouse for about three hours. It is a cold undertaking.

First I put on longjohns, then my trousers, then a turtleneck pullover sweater, and on top of all that something I once brought back from Sweden with those "milkman-mitten" sleeves.

It is not easy nowadays to find a pair of pants wide enough so that you can stuff your pockets full and squat.

Sometimes you see guys wriggling around simply to get a cigarette lighter out of their pockets.

And then those silly wide legs get caught on every thorn.

the shape of a full-grown deer and that of a young deer

Why would fashion want to force a mature fellow to wear a pair of tight boys'-style pants?

Coat on. Wynand's fur-lined boots and Jaap's Russian hat. Once in the tree, no matter how sharply the east wind is blowing the earflaps cannot come down, otherwise you cannot hear. And that is half the work.

Then I just hope to spot them once → (mostly I do not)

To be quite honest, I seldom see them even though I work hard at it. I cook up all kinds of schemes:
here I am one night, dragging along the intestines of a deer for many miles in order to lure the foxes.

Another scheme I tried lasted for about a week. I planned to use our old, gray Bantam chicken as a lure. After an hour or so in the tree seat everything got quiet and I pulled out Annie who, startled, began to squawk. I quickly put her back under my warm coat. Somehow during those nights we grew attached to each other and even found it peaceful and cozy with just the two of us amid the cold forest.

Almost always I sit there looking silly — with a wet, runny nose.

When you sit there waiting you must not make a single sound —
and that includes nose sniffing, too, so after a while I have a rock-hard ice mustache. It hurts sometimes when I silently have to yawn. Actually, it's all pure misery, but somehow it's worth it in the end.

When I get home, I have a large dish of warm rice, cooked in milk, with butter, sugar, and cinnamon added — at those times I for some reason have a craving for such childish foods.

After you sit there for awhile, your eyes get quite accustomed to the dark — you could practically read a book; and when an unsuspecting deer strolls past me, my happiness is almost too much — the way the Good Lord has created it all!

Or a little rabbit starts gnawing on a twig right next to me.

On three consecutive nights, when to attract the fox I was mimicking the frightened squeals of a rabbit, an owl settled in the tree right opposite me.
Noiselessly moving his head from side to side watching me all the time.
Marvelous!

One night after sitting in my spot for three hours I decided I had had enough, so I began walking home, wooden legged and staggering, not having seen a thing. It had been snowing continously and I was so thoroughly chilled that I felt numb (also the relief I so urgently needed was obtained by mere guesswork).

But wait; it seemed like a miracle. I had never seen anything so beautiful: suddenly the clouds parted and the moon shone through, even while it continued snowing! The effect was something like sunshine and rain simultaneously. For miles and miles no one was around, there was no disturbing light, and except for the soft rustling of the snowflakes there was not a single sound.

How is it possible to have had the fortune to be there and to witness this? "Praise the Lord from the heavens... for it is good to sing praises to our god!"

I just stood very still for a while: "Bless the Lord, O my soul — and all that is within me."

Overwhelmed by all that beauty I peacefully continued on my way home. I had to pass through a few hundred yards of fir trees, where I couldn't see a thing after coming from those moonlit moorlands. Dark and dead silent.
Then suddenly I got the fright of my life: a malicious roar and the sound of grinding teeth came from nearby, six feet away at the most. I guessed that it was some giant animal, angry because it had not heard me approaching, but through the heavy, drooping branches I could not discover anything. No tree was close enough to climb into. I didn't want to continue walking because he might think I was afraid.
So we both stood there: I, "bravely" talking in a loud voice all the time, and it, growling, and always that awful sound of those big teeth. Well, this went on for five long minutes. Finally I heard it leave with crackling noises through the woods. Every ten steps I stopped to listen—You never know...
I am no coward but this I don't like.

Last summer I also had an exciting few minutes. Suddenly on the way home a wild boar came charging out of the woods, aiming for Sep. It was a sow protecting her piglets — that's why.

We walked like this for quite a while.

Now and then she would pretend like she was going to attack, but fortunately nothing else happened.

These are not fellows to fool around with, especially when you see how they fight with each other.
↓

My way of hunting, all by myself, doesn't put much meat on the table. I don't mind. All the things I get to see this way are of inestimable value for an animal painter. (I prefer this to pheasant hunting for example. I don't care too much about that.)

It is not that I pity those pheasants or other wildfowl — No, I don't care much about it.

The lives of those millions of freezer chickens are pitiful — you get one half with your bami special (an Indonesian dish popular in Holland).

I drew these people at Foo Shan, where we go for dinner from time to time. They themselves added their names so you know too what they are called.

陳慧霞

張錦華

I am always amazed at how she manages to clear a table in one go with so many items.

侯家祥

It was a surprise when I looked in the mirror this morning. Yesterday I had received a bang on my head.

As a matter of fact, the day started wrong. I walked out of the door singing: "Dearest Jesus, we are here," and at once got a big blob of pigeon dropping down my neck.

Then I bent down to pick up something off the ground. At the same time Peer threw his head up — bang!

But do you know why I am so pleased? Not only because I still have my teeth, but also that I did not, on impulse, give Peer a whack. The animal meant no harm.

In the past I have done stupid things like that and regretted it for many years.

My brother Harm was walking sprightly with Amber the dog, when suddenly a hare crossed the road. Amber surged forward, dragging the little fellow along the gravel path. Harm's little knees were all torn up. I gave that dog hell!

Years later when the boys were romping around and one fell, Amber still cringed guiltily.

Regret!

Peer and Mr. Pastor have a new friend now: Gustur, an Icelandic pony, a seven-year-old gelding.

The three of them are so attached to one another that when Irene goes for a ride Peer whinnies to the sky until they return again.

Irene on Gustur

This is how we got the Icelander: over the phone Miss Boeke from Drente asked, "Do you know what you forgot in your Horses book?

The Icelandic pony."

Indeed I had. Stupid.

Says she: "And that's why I am going to give you an Icelandic foal!"

Well, that was very sweet of her!

We had no trouble falling in love with the Icelander, whom we named Gustur.

The Icelandic breed stems from ancient times, is winter hardy, content with little food, affectionate, and very strong — he can carry an adult with ease thirty miles a day or more!

For about a thousand years it has been strictly prohibited to import horses in Iceland.

An Icelandic equestrian who has participated in races on the mainland can of course return without any problem — but not his horse. He must sell it — they won't let it in under any circumstances. Consequently this little horse is one of the very few thoroughbreds.

You cannot change the fact of course that it looks a bit disproportionate to see a tall man on a small horse.

Nevertheless, I happily go for a ride every so often — sometimes delivering letters to Harm and Wieke, who live about four miles further on through the woods.

And we have more plans!

In Baarn I managed to get hold of this old cart.

There were some tense moments crossing the busy traffic stop near the palace with such a thing behind your car.

The cart has some really nice features

I don't have a harness yet, and it still remains to be seen whether Gustur will be amenable to that.

For his convenience I am taking lessons from Mr. Kraay, together with a few other people. He teaches us the Achenbach system of driving.

I even wind up the clock in the Achenbach technique now.

practicing with Fri

red deer
stock dove
collared turtle dove

I like tall grass.
I like to look at it.
I think it's fun to walk through,
and I like to draw it.

Last month I went to get some clumps of tall grass to liven up my view of the woodlands. That was quite some job. I had to dig up a big clod of earth with it and then push the whole heavy affair very carefully — the straws are very fragile — into my car.

Near our previous house I also had planted, with a lot of hard work, a similar area with that picturesque grass. When we returned from our holiday, my father-in-law, who likes to keep things neat, said:

"I have cut down that dry stuff nicely for you."

I also planted outdoors again the tree that was in our living room at Christmas. I am curious to see if it will take. Every year I get a Christmas tree at Sebo Detmers who, besides his paintings, also sells Christmas trees.

To make it a bit of a ceremonious occasion I collected the tree with Peer and Mr. Pastor. God willing, I'll do this every year from now on.

These bucks have similar kinds of antlers,

knob buck

but there is a difference: the deer on the left is a strong, healthy yearling buck and on the right is an old buck designated as game. You need to have had quite a number of years of experience to be able to distinguish the difference, especially when night is falling.

The differences are sometimes very small — the one on top is a game buck, but if you would shoot the one below you would commit a mortal sin:
it is a doe and, as the udder indicates, one having fawns.

↖ All these animals the layman calls for convenience' sake DEER.
Well, eleven of these are not just called deer. Crossword puzzles and newspaper reports are rather sloppy in giving names.

These are all different animals and you have to be sure which is which before you get involved with them. Poachers bang down anything they meet.

"Deer Rescued From Canal" That seems to me quite a tall story!

← Most of the time they mean a roe deer.

Such a shot animal — even if it is a runt or an old roebuck — is still a lot better off than, for example, a box calf. A buck like that has led a normal buck existence throughout his whole life with all the good and bad things, until he suddenly keeled over.

A box calf just → stands there waiting on his weak, unused little legs... not because the cattle farmer wants it but because the consumer likes that succulent, tender, white meat so much.

"The panting deer escaped from the hunt" of Psalm 42 that we sing does not exist here. Yes, I did see a panting deer that wasn't too steady on its legs, but that was at the end of the rutting season.

This way of hunting — just sitting and waiting motionless until the sought-after buck finally turns up — is for me as an animal painter ideal. You see so much more than when you go crashing through the woods.

I watch the behavior of the rabbits.

I see how the dove courts, with his wing over his girlfriend, and

how the roe hind nurses her fawn.

It happens sometimes that a little bird just can't stand the suspense any longer. It has to investigate the reason why I don't move.

And then there's that distinguished little whistle of the wren who, just by himself, sits there praising the Good Lord! ↓

A while ago sitting on my lookout seat I spotted something of which I couldn't make head nor tail. It was moving slightly up and down all the time. Only after peering through my binoculars for a long time did I figure it out: a pair of woman's boots with those silly platform soles!
The things you see sometimes!

The best time to observe wildlife is in the evening and early in the morning. In my earlier days I often slept in the woods overnight in order to be back in the tree before sunrise... not very cozy, especially with a downpour during the night.
One pitch-black night I heard someone or something making a smacking sound below me.
Although the chances of seeing something are smaller in the evening, no more early mornings for me. I no longer enjoy setting the alarm clock for 3:30 a.m. Besides being wide awake and more alert in the evening I am more observant.

Before the days when I slept in the woods, I sometimes stayed overnight in Arnold's cabin. That was no good either — as soon as I got up at the crack of dawn all those dogs started to make quite a racket! And then it was Arnold's turn, yelling from beneath his blankets, on top of all that.

Anyway, I really don't like staying with other people at all — you can end up in a little room where, with a great roar, the freezer switches on every thirty minutes...

I hate this toiling in the night.

or in a bed like this: as soon as I lay down, the mattress bulged up on either side of me so high that only my nose protruded above it. And then, very cautiously, in order not to make any noise, I made myself some kind of lair on the floor.

Just when I lay down again I felt a very urgent need to go! I had no idea of where the toilet was and it didn't feel right to stumble around in a strange house in the middle of the night. As it always happens in those cases: no washbasin, no vase, no flowerpot, no comb tray — nothing. And the skylight was at eye-level. I wouldn't make that.

Very, very quietly I unscrewed the ceiling light fixture. Creak, creak.

Then I poured it through the skylight.

I'd still rather stay in the woods — plenty of trees and bushes!

Besides, with what I have to do after awakening I can be sure that the buck won't venture on one, sometimes two trails. If you know what I mean.

No, I don't like this messing about.

Peer   Mr. Pastor   Gustur   Ko

I throw those rations into the feeding troughs and while they are eating I fetch an extra handful of hay. Then something happens to which I look forward every night: Ko is standing there, her fat hindquarters blocking access to the rack.

"KO, MOVE OVER PLEASE!"

It pleases me so much to say that and to know that it works! That this entire horse body wobbles aside! Just because you say
"Ko, move over please."
Terrific!
Ko is an Icelandic mare, six years old, a stout, cheerful girl with a sweet face.

This is what I am aiming for: Gustur and Ko together pulling the horse cart.
Maybe one day.

When Grandpa walked with me I always made sure which side I was on. The index finger from his left hand was missing (it had happened in the Boer War). On that side I definitely didn't want to hold hands with him.

↑ This small station has long since gone, and this path too.
Rural places have more or less disappeared in Schiedam. In nearby Kethel, where two of my brothers are living, there are still some picturesque corners.

Like here, for example, where my brother Harm lives. (I still intend to do a painting with a church in it and then affix a real clock onto the tower.) My brother Harm quite likes practical jokes. There are two posts in front of his house. But what you don't notice immediately is that they are made of rubber. And there is always someone who wants to use a post like that to lean his bike against or to play leap-frog over.

my brother Harm
(nice fellow)

My youngest brother Pit with Liesbet and Walter and Renée live in Soest, not far from us.
It's nice for getting together from time to time on Sunday for coffee after church.

And Pit and I often go on hikes. Regularly we shiver together on the lookout seat.

Lately we have been going horseback riding.

The first time this didn't go so smoothly. I was just thinking, "Well, Pit has courage!" He was enjoying a flying gallop through the sand dunes when Ko suddenly came to a dead stop.

Luckily Pit was unharmed.

This training cart I got from Monique de Roos who is expecting a baby and consequently cannot play with her horses anyway.

also a harness

Last Sunday I had Ko walk up and down the Black Path a few times, dragging this thing behind her. Not bad at all.

good girl, Ko

I am anxious to know when the right time will be to put her in front of the cart.

I had gone to the horse market to buy a couple of leather halters because I don't like those nylon ones. I really wasn't planning to buy anything else, but what do I see there?

A delightful little cart, like the ones cowboys used to ride to church on Sundays. I just couldn't resist.

After all, I don't care about going out to fancy places, nor about eating out, nor about sunbathing in the Caribbean. You will never see me standing in front of a show window of a men's fashion store, I don't care about having the latest model car,

but I am crazy about carts and harnesses.

I enjoy it already, pulling it myself.

If all is well — when this book is finished — I will sand this cart nicely and give it a coat of transparent varnish.

that flap!

For a week or two now we have had a couple of wild ducks (drake and female) in our pond. They came flying along — just like that.
We think it's nice and not so nice at the same time.
The nice part is obvious.
What is not so nice is that the water plants that are just about to emerge are being destroyed.

They seem to feel themselves quite at home. Just as if they belong here, they come waddling along when Corrie starts feeding the chickens and doves.

They don't worry too much about the dogs. At the most they may stretch their necks for a moment when a dog comes a little too close. But what I find remarkable is that Sep quietly ignores them.

At the duck hunt he is always gung-ho, peering intently into the sky, quivering with excitement.

And when I miss he starts to whine sadly because he just loves to retrieve ducks!

He likes it best of all when the shot duck drops down into the water — he enjoys turning it into a big event.

When Tok, somewhat further along, shoots a duck, Sep still brings it to me instead.

When nothing has happened for several hours Sep lies down in a dry ditch and starts to pant in an exaggerated manner.

Our feeding of the chickens and ducks attracts more and more turtle doves — more than I like to see.
But something *is* being done about it.
Tok just had a look outside and what did he see?
The sparrow hawk!

In the woodlands I had noticed earlier a place at the foot of a tree where there were lots of feathers.

Sometimes, from the corner of my eye, I see a shadow flitting through the trees.

The chickens run back home in a great hurry.

↑ the last pheasant hen

The attacker doesn't bother the chickens — they are too big for him.

One morning when there was a thin layer of snow on the ground I could clearly see cat prints all over the place!

A pity; I would have liked so much to have a pheasant hen with chicks.

Also it's not the sparrow hawk who has plucked my fifteen pheasants.

Flemish jays are not attacked by sparrow hawks; there are more than enough of them around the house.

For that job you need another kind of hawk, but you don't see them in this area.

a buzzard, which we do see here in the winter ↓

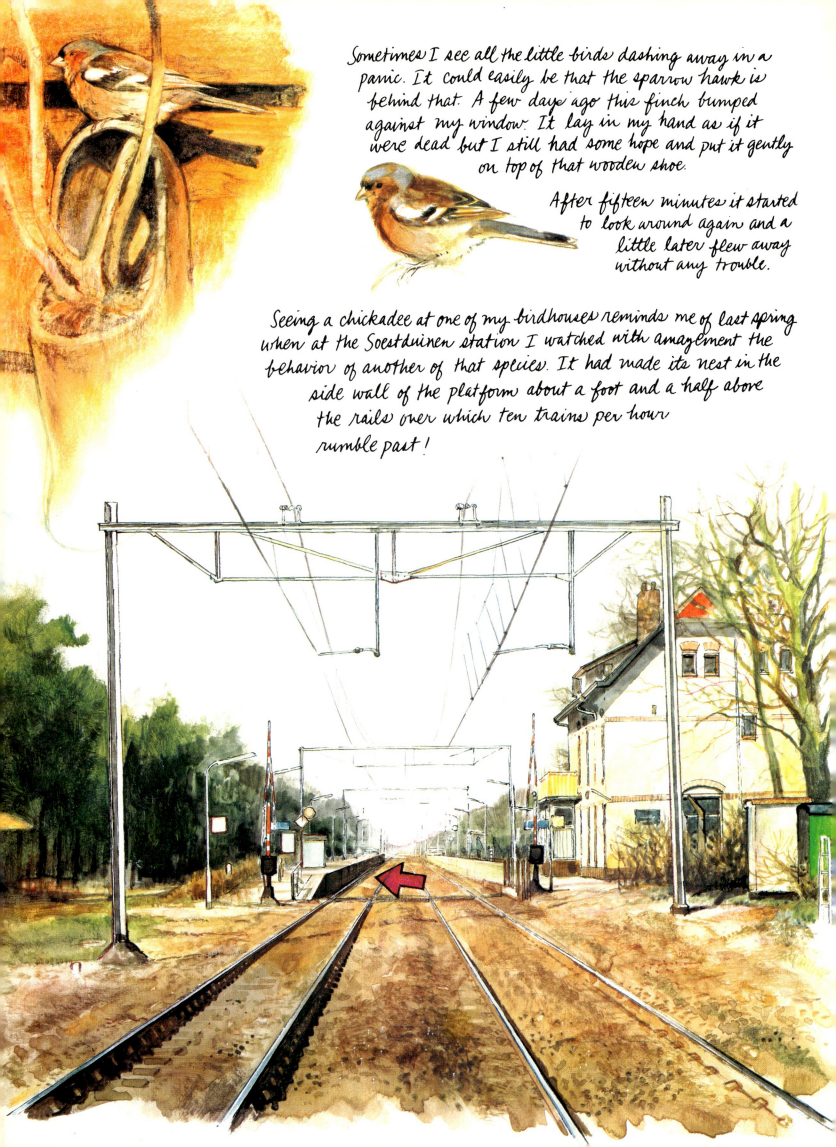

Sometimes I see all the little birds dashing away in a panic. It could easily be that the sparrow hawk is behind that. A few days ago this finch bumped against my window. It lay in my hand as if it were dead but I still had some hope and put it gently on top of that wooden shoe.

After fifteen minutes it started to look around again and a little later flew away without any trouble.

Seeing a chickadee at one of my birdhouses reminds me of last spring when at the Soestduinen station I watched with amazement the behavior of another of that species. It had made its nest in the side wall of the platform about a foot and a half above the rails over which ten trains per hour rumble past!

Animals often choose the most improbable spots: three days in a row I had to remove the nesting attempts of a wren — at night the stable door has to be closed!

This reminds me that for a long time I have intended to hang this nuthatch birdhouse in a better place. I just did it.

On the outside of the stable underneath the gutter I hung this cozy little teapot.

(It's a special house with two entrances alongside the tree trunk)

In the meantime the wild duck is sitting on her eggs! I had laid down an old milk can for her but she didn't seem to think much of it.

If this means that we will soon get little ducklings in our pond then we won't complain any longer about all the water plants that have disappeared.

One more example of strange breeding places: At the airfield Soesterberg I know of a fox's den about thirty feet from the runway!

Only this one is left — it probably didn't taste right.

It is now April 17 and suddenly things are happening terribly fast!

Small miracles all over the place.

I wanted to go out and pick yet another flower to draw, but I just noticed it started to rain. We can well use it.
So I'll put my painting equipment down and fertilize the meadow.

Well, that's another job done — sprinkling of fertilizer granules. That rain shower came in handy. You have to get the hang of that sprinkling — the arm doing the sprinkling goes forward at the same time as does the left leg.

This way it is open → and this way ↓ closed.

You stand there with open mouth, amazed at all the good Lord's creations!

← Brother Dirk Lam, who also supplies me with hay, did a demonstration using a saucepan with gravel.

You aim straight for a particular post, move over five steps, and back again.

There are quite a number of odd jobs that I've had to make time for: a milk can for the duck, hanging a teapot for the wren, stacking bales of hay, removing a few dead branches. I see Manasse lifting his leg over a newly planted seedling. I will have to put something around it.
It is difficult keeping the drawing paper clean after such jobs, because I don't like to wash my hands. Otherwise I quite enjoy doing a bit of carpentry. But I dislike it intensely when I am just four screws short, and have to go to the hardware store. Often you have to sit there for such a long time. I don't like wasting my day.

Do you know what I find so unfair? That in all stores the telephone always gets priority. You stand there dutifully on line and another person sitting comfortably on his easy chair gets all the information about the different types of lawn mowers, etc.

It is nice when children are so trusting with animals.

At the horse market I bought a small, flat saddle for Renée and Walter so now and then they mount Mr. Pastor — or as they call him, Mr. the Store.

When I see tiny toddlers playing with a life-size dog, I often wonder: Would we grownups have the guts?

In the meantime I've been making nice progress with Ko.

To teach a horse like that you have to train it with some kind of a drag.

← In action.

I came across that practical hint in an English manual. Just use two larch branches and nail a board over them — easy, safe, and cheap.

At Easter the weather was so tempting that I put Ko before the cart.
At first I walked behind it but when nothing alarming happened I jumped in. Of course we both have to learn a lot but the good intention is there.

Feeling like a king!

the first ride

disposable plastic ice cream spoon

I really dislike plastic.
I am really pleased I'm not the owner of a factory that, every single day, adds thousands of these nasty objects to the large heap of garbage there is already.
You know that children throw these things away carelessly.

Before I let the horses out in the meadow I'll wait for one more decent rain shower.
I have checked over the area:
one car wheel, five L.P. records, part of a bicycle and lots of plastic.

How easily people throw things away!

Although we hadn't moved into the new house yet I used to go there every day — even if it only was to stroll through the woods. One day I discovered to my horror that one of the construction workers had been defecating in my woods and had left many pages from the Yellow Pages scattered around.
Things like that infuriate me more than the fact that one of the painters accidentally broke the bathtub. I didn't mind that so much.

I must stop complaining now.

BLACK GROUSE FOR SALE!
In September and October I am selling about one hundred of my black grouse. With or without clipped wings. Best offers. Address letter to the newspaper office, using code nr. A31764

I couldn't get to sleep last night, because of that ad in Avicultura.

Wouldn't that be fantastic in the woodlands? I dreamed about them all night.

The cats, however...

Do you know what else I dream from time to time? That the great John Sebastian Bach is listening to his own masterworks three centuries later. I don't know why I have that dream, but praise the Lord that Bach once existed!

Bach made a few serious attempts to meet his contemporary Handel, but to Bach's deep sorrow Handel didn't care.

That still bothers me.

I often wonder what the Lord will think when He returns and sees what we have made of the world.

Said Udo Saathof when I found him in tears sitting on the staircase— he had been ordered to his room, after everything had gone wrong, and received a good hiding—
"I wish that the Lord Jesus would come back. Life isn't so great this way."

And he is right.

I just took the flag and the pennon down from the attic because tomorrow is April 30, Queen Juliana's birthday.

Horst Reetz wanted to demonstrate what a marvelous sense of smell his dog had. He dug a coin out of his pocket and threw it far away into the woods. The dog retrieved it without hesitation!

But here is the nice part of the story:

A farmer, while mowing, had fortunately noticed that a newborn fawn was lying in the tall grass and carefully circumvented that area.

Then the same dog was led to the clump of grass in which the fawn was lying, but he didn't notice anything!

The Good Lord has arranged it all so wisely: a newborn fawn doesn't give off any scent.

At a distance I lay in waiting. When it got dark the mother came to fetch it.

It is amazing that there is a little fellow like this sitting in this water — an airtight package! That's really another of God's miracles. Just because we have known for a long time how this works, it shouldn't prevent us from openly marveling at these things.

Yesterday morning (May 12) they finally hatched: seven. Hardly half an hour in the world and they are skimming in a zigzag on the water chasing a mosquito.

How is it possible?

Such a brand-new duckling is already a good-looking little guy, but most chirpers I hear everywhere in the birdhouses are no more than promissory notes.

A nuthatch has taken over one of the chickadee houses, in spite of the fact that I made a special nuthatch birdhouse that is hanging empty. Then I thought maybe I made a mistake. It could be that the tree trunk is too smooth to give a good grip for those tiny nails.

During the whole period the duck sat on the eggs the drake stopped by about three times a day. But since the ducklings were born we haven't seen him.

At first we were worried about how the dogs would take to them. Very well, indeed.

Tim, out of curiosity, came just a little too close and was attacked. He yelped as if he were caught in a door.

Since that time the dogs completely ignore the family.

So the mother duck need not fear our dogs, but she has to keep an eye open for crows, which, from time to time, come to have a look at the little ones.

A comic sight — a duck looking up. It has to be done in this way because a duck cannot look straight ahead.

So many things are happening in the month of May!
One moment there's nothing, then suddenly there's everything!
It all happens very quickly: animals, flowers, leaves

One wonders where it all comes from.

blossoms

cows in the meadow

Peer, Mr. Pastor, Ko, and Gustur are out in the meadow again.
We are lucky that in our country we have four seasons and that in turn it will look like this.
I really don't know which one I find the most beautiful.

This is the view you get from the tower in Soest when you look in the direction of Spakenburg.

I marvel at the ease with which a little jackdaw like this just lets itself drop from the balustrade. I even find it a bit scary just to lean against it.

the pump

The climb to the top of the tower had another advantage. Looking around I discovered in the neighborhood of Black Willem on the Eem a herd of pigs comfortably relaxing with their fat hindquarters in the warm sand.
 I must go over there soon.

Because calves and most pigs spend their lives in those miserable feedlots, we don't eat any veal or pork, only old cows.

This does not mean, however, that we wouldn't enjoy eating some porkchops. I will go to that farmer and inquire about the possibility of buying half a pig.

Wouldn't it be nice if all calves could walk around like this...

This dovecote belongs to the cheese factory next to Farmer Lam. I want to make something similar out of the Marienburg tower.

That is one of the many odd jobs I plan to do, God willing, when this book is finished.

Another job I look forward to is fixing up this cart.

The cart has the type of axles that need greasing, so in anticipation I bought a bucket of grease at Jurriaans. He simply uses his bare hands to pull that black goo out of the tub.

From Jurriaans I go straight to Corrie de Bruin's for pipe tobacco. All done. Now I can go home and continue working.

I don't like shopping and certainly not when I have to wait.

Last week I drove Corrie, Liesbet, and Wieke to Bunschoten-Spakenburg — they wanted to buy sewing material. On no account would I go into the stores with them. I would rather hang around outside for an hour.

I'm really so pleased to see so many women in traditional costume in that area.

Paintings of water can, of course, be beautiful; that's not the point. It's quite a difficult task to do it well — at least I think it is.

For example, stagnant water with some reflections is fairly easy to paint, but when you have to add those ripples it's hard.

By the way, the pleasure of having those ducklings in our pond was short-lived. After four days the whole family disappeared, and we haven't seen them since.

The birdhouses are empty again. When checking I found them full of horsehair. In one of them was this dead fledgling. Just look at those curious mouth corners — it looks like a hammerhead shark.

Drawing a simple cage like this takes much more time than you might imagine.

For comparison, I think it took me four times as long to put this on paper than this little bird.

But what I really want to say is that soon Gijs will be allowed to leave his cage and be put outside in his summer residence.

A few years ago I made this outdoor cage for Gijs with all kinds of interesting branches in it. At last a more exciting life for him! But there he sits all summer in the same spot; in fact he hardly moves at all!

In a way I regret the wasted effort but then I won't have to feel sorry for him when he has to go indoors again in the fall. I wear a work glove when I go to catch him — he can cut your fingers off!

I hate to see animals being kept in cages that are too small. In the old days people didn't consider such things. When we got married we bought ourselves a Mozambique siskin. The sweet little creature (the size of my little finger) has been sitting in this cage near the window for **21** years.

This you often see too: a Japanese nightingale in a miserable small cage — hop-hop, back and forth all the time, day in, day out.

The cage should depend, of course, on the type of animal. A few white mice are quite happy in an old aquarium like this, if they have something to do.

Gerbils and hamsters can be kept in the same way.

During my childhood, gerbils and hamsters were not kept as pets. The golden hamster was only discovered in 1930 in Syria, and I had to smuggle my first hamster across the border from Germany.

Willem Buys smuggled into the country for me the very first apricot-colored hamster.

(Willem and I worked for many years together at the advertising agency Lintas)

I gave once some pieces of pink knitting wool to an expectant mother mouse for nesting material. But that resulted in violent quarrels — in every tail she saw a piece of knitting wool! Even her own tail was carried to the nest from time to time.

The day before yesterday, I saw in the woodlands the pink dormouse. (Just like the ones you always see in gnome dwellings!)

Every day I find pieces of glass on the ground. After each walk I throw a handful of glass into the trash can. I get the feeling that in earlier days people used the woods as a place to throw away broken bottles and such things.

Mrs. van de Woude gave me this lovely Salvation Army hat. My wife calls something like that a "sweetie."

Willem Hey in Hillegom cultivated this Allium (onion family) and named it after me.

It's at least as successful as this old trusted broad-brimmed bonnet.

Only that emblem...↑ This hat deserved better. Those strange slanting letters remind me of the Persian tablecloth draped diagonally over the small cloister table.

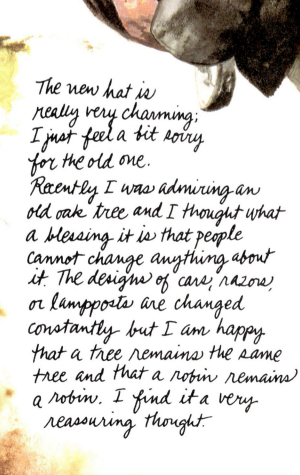

The new hat is really very charming; I just feel a bit sorry for the old one.
Recently I was admiring an old oak tree and I thought what a blessing it is that people cannot change anything about it. The designs of cars, razors, or lampposts are changed constantly but I am happy that a tree remains the same tree and that a robin remains a robin. I find it a very reassuring thought.

I am delighted that designers cannot change the appearance of wild animals.

Just imagine: maybe a roebuck would look like this ↙ until you got bored with it, and then for a few years it would look like this.  But then comes the unavoidable change to the NEW! So, quickly something else again.

Conservative as I am I paint him like this. I cannot do it differently, and I don't want to. Trying to contain him in triangles I find too limiting, and the animal is too precious to me for that.
To render him true to nature is my greatest pleasure.

That can be done in many ways — like this or like this ↓

Saint Nicholas lives on the estate Madril, so not in or near Madrid — you would never find him there. The misunderstanding probably occured from the worn-out lettering on the steamboat.

Storage areas for toys, wrapping paper, gingernuts, gingerbread cookies, etc. ↓

the saint's palace Castle Madril ↓

← chapel

← Black Peter's house

stable →

← paddock with exercise roofs
← These barns are full of toys that don't work

Last night after supper, when I went out to the woods to get some fresh air, I was able to get very close to a roe deer hind. This doesn't happen very often, and I can't think of anything I'd rather do than observe such an unsuspecting animal at close quarters. When a foraging roe deer calmly strolls away so that I can get up without startling it, I am overjoyed!

For a long time I have wanted to try out something that offers a better chance for successful stalking.

This morning I also saw without being seen. I was just about to go up to the mailman to get the mail — when suddenly he put his bicycle against the gate and relieved himself.

I thought it best to hide myself behind a tree.

Suddenly I know what I'm going to do after this book and I'm already enthusiastic about it:
I will make animal models out of clay.

When I started this book I had no idea what it was going to look like. When I look through the pile of drawings, after working on it for almost a year, I see a confused picture book with neither head nor tail...
That's the way it is.
But this has to be absolutely the last page.
It is a pity that the book is finished.
But no complaining. I had a marvelous time working on it, so Praise the Lord!